Mel Bay's First Lessons
Mandolin
by Dix Bruce

All photos by Gene Tortora.

CD CONTENTS

1 Intro [:13]	22 John Henry/regular [1:05]	43 Buffalo Gals/slow [:48]
2 How to Tune [1:10]	23 My Home's Across the Blueridge Mountains/slow [:59]	44 Buffalo Gals/regular [:35]
3 Tuning [1:51]	24 My Home's Across the Blueridge Mountains/regular [1:09]	45 Oh, Them Golden Slippers/slow [1:36]
4 First Chords [1:30]	25 Seventh Blues/slow [:43]	46 Oh, Them Golden Slippers/regular [1:08]
5 Skip to My Lou/slow [:37]	26 Seventh Blues/regular [1:04]	47 Soldier's Joy/slow [1:22]
6 Skip to My Lou/regular [1:21]	27 Go Down Moses/slow [1:16]	48 Soldier's Joy/regular [:59]
7 Careless Love/slow [1:05]	28 Go Down Moses/regular [:57]	49 East Virginia/slow [:39]
8 Careless Love/regular [1:27]	29 Sometimes I Feel Like a Motherless Child/slow [1:11]	50 East Virginia/regular [:53]
9 Blue Tail Fly/slow [:56]	30 Sometimes I Feel Like a Motherless Child/regular [:55]	51 East Virginia/slow fill [:39]
10 Blue Tail Fly/regular [1:14]	31 First Melody [:48]	52 East Virginia/regular fill [:54]
11 Red River Valley/slow [:47]	32 Camptown Races/slow [:56]	53 Roving Gambler/slow [:58]
12 Red River Valley/regular [:52]	33 Camptown Races/regular [:38]	54 Roving Gambler/regular [:42]
13 Billy Boy/slow [:45]	34 Just a Closer Walk With Thee/slow [1:16]	55 Bluegrass Chop [1:53]
14 Billy Boy/regular [:55]	35 Just a Closer Walk With Thee/regular [1:46]	56 Roll in My Sweet Baby's Arms/slow [:40]
15 In the Pines/slow [:50]	36 My Walking Cane/slow [:53]	57 Roll in My Sweet Baby's Arms/regular [:47]
16 In the Pines/regular [1:10]	37 My Walking Cane/regular [1:10]	58 This Train/slow [:49]
17 St. James Infirmary/slow [:46]	38 The Great Speckled Bird/slow [:53]	59 This Train/regular [:56]
18 St. James Infirmary/regular [:56]	39 The Great Speckled Bird/regular [1:22]	60 Tremolo [:58]
19 Poor Wayfaring Stranger/slow [2:02]	40 Lonesome Valley/slow [:57]	61 Greensleeves/slow [1:27]
20 Poor Wayfaring Stranger/regular [1:38]	41 Lonesome Valley/regular [1:14]	62 Greensleeves/regular [1:10]
21 John Henry/slow [:57]	42 Eighth notes [:55]	

1 2 3 4 5 6 7 8 9 0

It doesn't get any easier.....

Visit us on the Web at www.melbay.com — E-mail us at email@melbay.com

Contents

Introduction

Hello and welcome! "First Lessons Mandolin" teaches the absolute basics of learning to play mandolin. We'll cover everything from holding the pick to performing easy mandolin tunes. It doesn't get any easier than this! You'll learn basic picking technique, how to tune the mandolin, all the most important mandolin chords, how to play easy melodies in several musical styles, and much more. Our main goal is to get you up and playing the mandolin as quickly as possible and to help you to have fun doing it! Let's get started!

Dix Bruce

The Mandolin and its Parts

Your mandolin is probably similar to one of two basic models: "a" style or "f" style. If you're playing a roundback or "taterbug," its face will be similar to the "a" model. Take a look at the diagram below and familiarize yourself with the different parts of the mandolin. Read through the text and find out why these parts are important. You should know the difference between your headstock and your endpin. You can always refer back to this diagram as we explore the mandolin in more depth in the text.

1. Bridge. Strings rest on the bridge, which conducts their vibration to the resonant top of the mandolin. Nearly all mandolin bridges "float," held onto the top only by the tension of the strings. As such, bridges move and may need to be corrected periodically to insure proper intonation. Some bridges are height adjustable by two small wheels imbedded in the bridge itself.

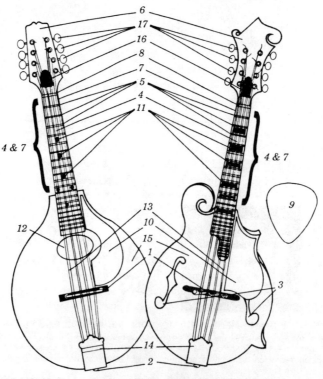

2. Endpin. The endpin holds one end of your strap. If you have an F-style mandolin, the other end of the strap goes around the curl. If your mandolin doesn't have a curl, tie the other end onto the headstock (6), under the strings near the nut (8).

3. F-Hole. F-holes are shaped like a script letter F as on a violin. After the music goes round and round, it comes out here. Other mandolins, like the A-style, have oval-shaped sound holes (see diagram #3 & #12).

4. Fretboard or Fingerboard. This is where your fingers press the strings to make different notes and chords. Always place your fretting finger in the space between the metal frets, not on the metal frets themselves.

5. Frets. Frets are the actual metal wires that delineate the fret spaces. When we refer to "fret one" we mean the space between the nut and the first fret wire. When we refer to "fret two" we mean the space between the first and second fret wires. Remember, put your fingers in the space, not on the fretwire!

6. Headstock. The headstock holds the tuning gears (17) which anchor one end of the strings. The other end of the strings, which have a loop, are anchored to the tailpiece (14).

7. Neck. The neck connects the headstock with the body of the instrument and holds the fingerboard and strings. "The neck bone's connected to the headstock…"

8. Nut. The other point, besides the bridge, where the strings rest. The nut sits between the headstock and the end of the fingerboard and is slotted so the strings don't wander. It's usually made of bone or ivory.

9. Pick. The pick or plectrum is the little piece of plastic you use to contact the strings when you strum or play single notes to make noise/music. Picks come in a variety of shapes, sizes, and thicknesses. Get several to try out. Stay away from thin picks.

10. Pickguard. A pick guard protects the top of your mandolin from pick scratches and gouging.

11. Position Markers. These are the mother-of-pearl or painted dots and decorations on the front and side of the fingerboard which help you tell, at a glance, one fret from another. You'll usually find them on frets five, seven, nine, twelve and fifteen. Fret twelve usually has two. Most mandolins also have markers on the side of the neck so you can tell positions with a side-long glance.

12. Soundhole. The oval-shaped opening on A-type mandolins. See #3. F-hole above.

13. Strings. The mandolin has eight strings tuned in pairs to the same pitches as violin strings: E-A-D-G, from highest to lowest pitch, from right to left as you look at the fingerboard. Strumming or picking the strings makes them vibrate. These vibrations are in turn amplified by the top of the instrument. (By the way, they're not really strings at all, they're wires.)

14. Tailpiece and Cover. This is where the loop ends of the strings not attached at the headstock are anchored. Strings often rattle and buzz here. To remedy this, weave a thin piece of leather or felt through the strings, between the bridge and tailpiece. If the tailpiece cover rattles, weave a thin piece of leather or felt between the tailpiece and tailpiece cover.

15. Top or Soundboard. The top is the main vibrating element of the mandolin. It has to be strong enough to survive the tremendous pressure the strings exert on it, while supple enough to easily resonate and amplify the string vibrations. The quality of the top, a trade-off between strength and resonance, most determines the quality of the sound of the instrument.

16. Truss Rod Cover. Many mandolins have necks reinforced with a metal truss rod. Most of these rods are adjustable (best done by a repair professional) under the truss rod cover, to correct the neck warp that time, weather, and string pressure often cause. The truss rod cover is a plate, usually plastic, which cosmetically covers this adjustment point.

17. Tuning Gears. Tuning gears tighten or loosen string tension to raise or lower the pitch of the strings to tune the mandolin.

Your mandolin should sound fairly good and be relatively easy to play though it may be difficult for you to tell at this point. And, if you're a complete beginner just about everything can seem difficult to play and may not sound good! It would be worth your while to consult a local instrument repair person to make sure that your mandolin is set up well enough to give you a fighting chance at playing it.

I always recommend that students play with a strap. A strap will help you maintain a constant playing position whether you are sitting or standing. (See position photos right & below.) Your mandolin should have an endpin protruding from the bottom of the body, opposite from the headstock, around which one end of your strap will attach. As I mentioned in #2 above, if you have an F-style mandolin, the other end of the strap goes around the curl. If your mandolin doesn't have a curl, tie the other end onto the headstock (6), under the strings near the nut (8). My strap is a simple and thin piece of leather. You can make your own from stock bought at a leather or shoe shop. Commercial straps usually have adjusting buckles. It's best to avoid this type of strap as they'll bang against your mandolin and scratch it.

Holding the mandolin

Balance your mandolin gently with your fretting hand. Lightly place the thumb on the side of the back of the neck (the mandolin's, not yours!). Your fingers should reach around to the fingerboard. The strap should go all the way around both of your shoulders, not just off the one. Bluegrassers tend to use the "one shoulder" technique which developed because most of the early mandolin and banjo players wore hats and they would have had to take their hat off to put the strap over their head. While the one shoulder technique is convenient hat-wise, it can lead to a lot of tension and stress as that shoulder holds the mandolin in position.

Balancing the mandolin

Left hand position, side view

Whether you're sitting or standing, find comfortable and relaxed positions for your upper body and arms. Everybody feels a little tight at first, but your ultimate goal is to relax your shoulder, arm, and hand muscles so there's a minimum of stress in those areas. The less stress, the easier it will be to play and the longer you'll be able to play.

When you fret strings, make contact with the tips of your fingers. Over time you'll develop calluses on your fretting fingertips and this is a good thing. Your fingertips will get sore in the process but that means that calluses are in the making. On some of the chord photos it may look as though my fingers are getting dangerously close to the fret wires. Since we're friends, I'll admit something to you: I have big fat fingers and big fat fingertips. However, I've developed healthy calluses on my fingertips and have learned how to place them in the frets so I get a nice clean ringing sound without thuds or buzzes. So, if I can do it with my fingers, you can do it with yours! It just takes a little practice.

Fingertip contact

Mandolins are tuned like violins, except that violins only have one string of each pitch; mandolins have two. Each string in the pair is tuned to the notes shown below. Tune to the tones at the beginning of the CD, use an electronic tuner, or tune to the piano. Listen to the "How to Tune" and "Tuning" tracks on the CD for tips on how to tune. Tuning notes on the piano are shown below. Start with string #1, the E, and get one of the pair in tune to your source, then tune the other in the pair to it. Move on to the next string and so on.

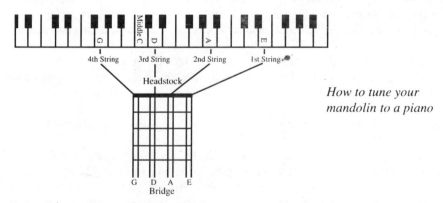

How to tune your mandolin to a piano

Getting your mandolin in tune requires lots of practice and listening. Be sure to work on it every time you play the instrument. It will develop over time. If you can't hear what's in tune yet, don't worry about it, but have someone help you tune your mandolin from time to time.

If you don't have access to any reliable tuning tones, you can still get your mandolin in tune with itself. First you have to decide which of the strings is most in tune and tune the others to it. Let's assume that the first string E (far right as you look at the fingerboard) is the closest to being correct. Fret the second string (A) at the seventh fret and match that fretted sound of the second string to the sound of the open first string. When these match you'll have strings one and two in tune. Now fret the third string (D) at the seventh fret and match that fretted sound to the sound of the newly tuned open second string. Finally fret the fourth string (G) at the seventh fret and match that fretted sound to the sound of the newly tuned open third string. Use this "fretted/open string" method whenever you need to check your tuning.

Let's Play!

You can make music on the mandolin one of two general ways: 1) strumming chords; or by 2) picking individual notes. We're going to start out with chords.

A chord is three or more tones played simultaneously. Since we only have four strings on the mandolin, the maximum number of notes we can have in a chord is four. A guitar has six strings so the maximum number of notes we can have in a guitar chord is six. A full sized piano has eighty eight keys so, theoretically, we could play a piano chord with up to eighty eight notes. But enough of these mind numbing possibilities.

Chords are important because most pop, country, jazz, bluegrass, gospel, rock, blues, folk, and about any other kind of music you can name, use chords to accompany a melody, which can be played on another instrument or sung. Within each genre these chords are fairly predictable and apply to hundreds of thousands of songs. Yes, I meant to say *hundreds of thousands of songs*. When you have learned just a few chords, you will be able to play thousands of easy songs. With a little more work and a more chords you'll be able to handle tens of thousands and so on. So, chords are very important to learn and the payoff will come almost immediately.

Chords are named with letters and suffixes like A, G, F, F7, Bb7, Gm, Am, Em. Each chord name gives us a specific recipe that describes which notes make up that given chord. We won't go into too much more depth than that but if you're interested in further study, check out my "You Can Teach Yourself Mandolin." (MB94331) For more specific music theory, try my "How to use a Capo, How to Transpose, and the Nashville Numbering System." (MB98413) Both are from Mel Bay.

Chords with a simple letter name like C, F, G, Bb ("B-flat"), Eb, are major chords and we'll learn several of them first. Chords named with letters followed by an "m" identify minor chords: Dm ("D-minor"), Gm, C#m ("C-sharp minor"). Minor chords have a somewhat "darker" sound than majors. Both simple major and minor chords have only three different notes in them and are called "triads." Chords named with letters followed by a "7" identify seventh or dominant seventh chords. In more advanced pop music and jazz you'll encounter 9s, 6s, 13s and more. You may also run into chords that are named with a mixture of letters and numbers like Gm7 ("G-minor seven") or C7b5 ("C-seven flat five"). All describe a specific set of notes for the chord.

We'll learn chords from photos and chord diagrams like the ones shown below. For the first few chords we'll show both the photo and chord diagram, then just the diagrams. Once you learn to read diagrams, you won't need the photos. Once you memorize the chords, you won't even need the diagrams!

The vertical lines of the chord diagram represent the strings on your mandolin, right to left, strings one through four. The horizontal lines represent the fret wires. The numbers in the grid tell us which fingers to use to fret the individual strings. Fretting finger numbers are as follows: 1 = index; 2 = middle; 3 = ring; 4 = pinkie. If you see a little "x" below or above one of the strings, don't play that string.

It's important that you memorize chords as you are introduced to them. Chords are like words and you'll need to build a vocabulary of them in order to speak musically. We'll teach you chords on easy, familiar songs. That will allow you to concentrate on learning the shapes, names, and sounds of the chords without having to worry about too much else. As I mentioned above, once you can play just a few chords and understand how to read chord diagrams you'll be able jump right in and play songs in just about any style. You'll be able to read chords from any source: guitar or piano books from your favorite bands — anything that includes chords — and play along. Even lyric sheets from the internet. By the way, I have downloadable mandolin music with chords and tablature posted on my website: www.musixnow.com

Unless you're reading from a book specifically designed for mandolin players, the music will probably not show you the actual mandolin chord diagrams like the ones shown below. If you memorize the chords, you won't find that to be a limitation. That's because a G chord on the piano is the same as a G on the guitar or the mandolin! Sure, you finger them differently, but as I said, they are all G chords or Cm chords, or B7 chords. It's really that simple and that's simply amazing! So memorize those mandolin chords!

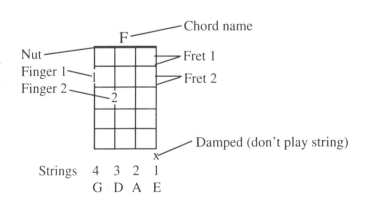

Photo of F chord

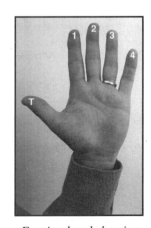

Fretting hand showing finger numbers

How to use the CD

The number one best thing you can do to learn chords is to play! One of the easiest and best ways to practice playing is to play along with me on the CD. Listen before you play. Every song will be there at two speeds; slow and regular. Practice the chords a bit on your own and then work your way up to the slow version on the CD.

Musical examples include rhythm guitar, which is panned to the stereo left channel. The part being taught and demonstrated on the recording is panned to the right channel. For the first part of the book where you're learning chords, melodies will be panned in the center. Later, when you're learning melodies, the mandolin chord rhythm will appear in the center, the mandolin melody will be panned to the right. By adjusting the balance control on your stereo, you can isolate the parts for study or play along.

It may be difficult for you to play along with the CD, especially in the beginning, so be patient and work your way up first to the slow version of each song, then to the regular speed version. Use the CD to first demonstrate how each song should sound, then as you progress, play along with the CD to master chords and melodies. One of the nice features of a CD is that you can set it up to automatically repeat a track as many times as you wish. Doing this will help build your strength, endurance, and speed.

It may take you awhile to be able to play at the regular speed version but the best thing you can do is play, play, play! Everyday is best. If you can only manage fifteen minutes the first few days, that's OK, just keep trying to play longer each day. Playing along with me on the CD will build up your strength and get you used to playing with other people.

As you work through these songs, it's important that you sing along in order to get the feel for the tune and how the melody (what you sing) fits with the accompaniment (the chords you play). Don't be shy, throw back your head and sing along with the CD! Try to play through all the verses to a song on your own. Since we are limited to 74 minutes on a CD, we can only include one or two verses. But, the more verses you sing and play, the faster you will progress and the more verses you learn the more you'll have to perform.

First Chords

The first two chords we're going to learn are the C and the G on the old folk song "Skip to My Lou." This is a simple and familiar song to get you used to strumming chords. Look at the two chords in the diagrams below. Practice holding the chords and strumming the strings with a light brush from the pick. Start slowly and strum each chord eight times. Play your strums slow enough so that you don't stop or break the rhythm of your strums as you change chords. Listen to the "First Chords" track on the CD.

C

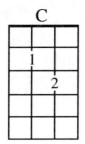 

G

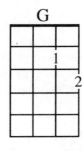 

Note how similar the C and G chords are shaped. To play the G, you simply move the C "over" one string. Because of the way the mandolin is tuned, you'll find that much about it is very regular and logical. Eventually you will be able to learn chords or melody, and easily move them up and down the fretboard or from string to string to different keys. You can't do that on a guitar. Reason #1 that the mandolin is superior to the guitar!

Hold the pick loosely in your picking hand. You only need to apply enough pressure to hold onto it as you strum. No doubt it will fly out of your hand from time to time but this will help you determine how much pressure is enough. Again, as with your shoulders and arms, you want to keep your picking hand as loose as possible. Stress will only cause fatigue and cramping and will slow you down.

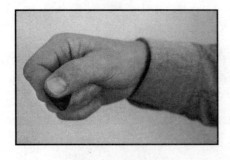

Holding the Pick

Picking the Strings— Two views

6

As we practice chords, we'll generally use single down strums. Of course there is a whole world of other strums and patterns you can use on the mandolin. Experiment with them yourself. We explore them in greater detail in "You Can Teach Yourself Mandolin."

Right & Left Hand Positions

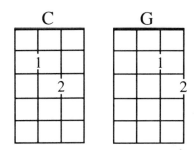

Skip to My Lou

1. Lost my part - ner what'- ll I do? Lost my part - ner what'- ll I do?
2. Flies in the butter milk, shoo, shoo, shoo, Flies in the butter milk, shoo, shoo, shoo,

Lost my part - ner what'- ll I do? Skip to my Lou my dar - ling.
Flies in the butter milk shoo, shoo, shoo,

Lou, Lou, skip to my Lou, Lou, Lou, skip to my Lou,

Lou, Lou, skip to my Lou, Skip to my Lou my dar - ling.

In "Careless Love," we'll use the G and C chords you already learned and add a new chord to it, the D.

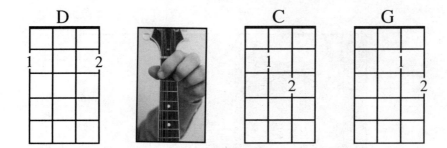

Careless Love

1. Love,   oh   love,   oh   Care - less   Love, _____
2. Sor - row,   sor - row   to   my   heart, _____

Love,   oh   love,   oh   Care - less   Love, _____
Sor - row,   sor - row   to   my   heart, _____

Love,   oh   love,   oh   Care -   less   Love,
Sor - row,   sor -   row   to   my   heart,

See   what   love   has   done   to   me. _____
Since   my   true   love's   been   a - part. _____

"Blue Tail Fly" uses the C and G chords plus a new one, the F. Remember that the small "x" under string one means that you should not play that string. I usually dampen it with my fretting hand or avoid it when I strum. The F chord looks like the G and C chords moved over one more string.

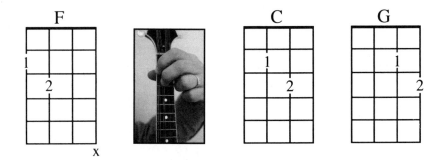

The Blue Tail Fly

Verse

1. When I was young I used to wait, On my old mas-ter and hold his plate, And
   when he'd ride in the af - ter - noon, I'd fol - low with a hicor - y broom, The

pass the jug when he got dry, And brush a - way the blue tail fly.
po - ny be - ing ver - y shy, When bit - ten by the blue tail fly.

Chorus

Jim-my crack corn and I don't care, Jim - my crack corn and I don't care,

Jim - my crack corn and I don't care, My mas - ter's gone a - way. 2. And

          C   F
3. One day they rode a-round the farm,
       C   G
The flies all over them did swarm.
       C   F
One chanced to bite him on the thigh.
       G   C
The devil take the blue-tail fly. (Chorus)

4. That pony run, he jump, he pitch,
He tumble master in the ditch,
He died and the jury wondered why,
The verdict was the blue-tail fly. (Chorus)

5. They laid him under a 'simmon tree,
His epitaph is there to see,
"Beneath this stone I'm forced to lie,
A victim of the blue-tail-fly." (Chorus)

9

As previously mentioned, in the course of "First Lessons Mandolin" we'll explore several different kinds of chords including seventh and minor chords. Let's look now at the C7 and G7 on "Red River Valley." Seventh and minor chords have a different combination of notes than their major brothers and sisters. Compare the differences between the C and C7 and the G and G7 chords. Notice that one note is different in each case, C to C7; G to G7. Also notice that the C7 looks like the G7 moved over one string. What do you think the F7 will look like?

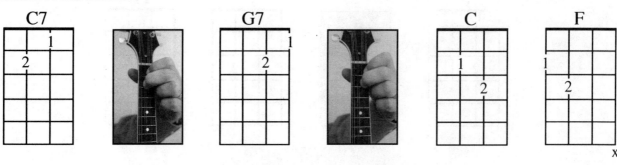

Red River Valley

1. From this val - ley they say you are go - ing, _____ We will
2. I've been think - ing a long time my dar - ling, _____ Of the

miss your bright eyes and sweet smile, _____ For they
sweet words you nev - er would say, _____ Now a -

say you are tak - ing the sun - shine, _____ That has bright - ened our
las must by fond hopes all van - ish? _____ For they say you are

path - ways a - while. _____ Come and sit by my side if you
go - ing a - way. _____

love me, _____ Do not has - ten to bid me a - dieu, _____

_____ Just re - mem - ber the Red Ri - ver Val - ley, _____

_____ And the cow - boy who loved you so true. _____

"Billy Boy" has a new chord: the A. Notice that the shape of the A has some elements of the G chord in it but moved up two frets. We've switched around the finger assignments and added two fretted notes. Notice that on the A you'll need to fret two strings with one finger. You may be able to use the tip of your first finger to cover both strings like I do. Otherwise, lay the pad of your finger (fingerprint down) across both strings. There will be more chords like this on the next few pages. Do your best play them as shown, otherwise use the finger pad or add a finger.

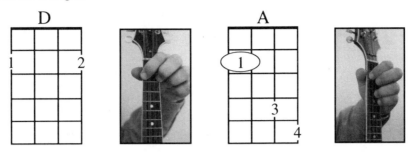

Billy Boy

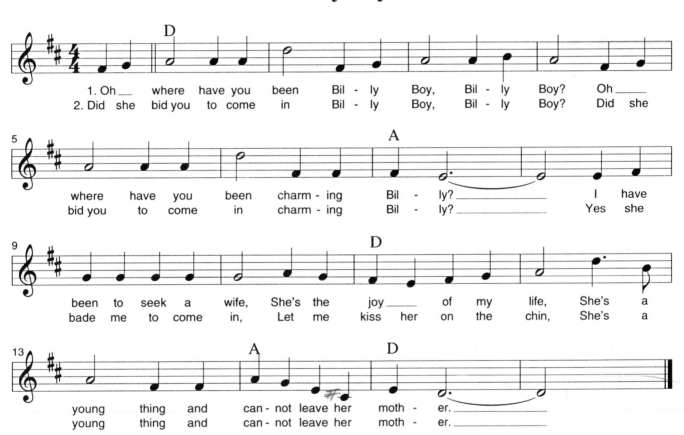

D
3. Can she bake a cherry pie, Billy Boy, Billy Boy,
                                 A
Can she bake a cherry pie, charming Billy?
A
She can bake a cherry pie,
             D
Quick as a cat can wink her eye,
                   A   D
She's a young thing and cannot leave her mother.

4. How old is she, Billy Boy, Billy Boy,
How old is she, charming Billy?
Three times six and four times seven,
Twenty-eight and eleven,
She's a young thing and cannot leave her mother.

"In the Pines" was recorded by the most famous mandolin player in the world, Bill Monroe, who, incidentally invented bluegrass music in the mid-1940s. The new chords are E and B7. As with the A chord, you'll need to fret two strings with one finger. If that's impossible on the E, try using adding the third finger on the second string, second fret. On B7 you can add the fourth finger on the first string second fret. By now you should be able to read the chord grids without the photos. All chords are listed alphabetically in the Chord Dictionary at the end of the book.

In the Pines

2. I asked my captain for the time of day,
         E   A   E
He said he throwed his watch away,
        B7   E
A long steel rail and a short cross tie,
        A   E
I'm on my way back home.
        B7   E

3. Little girl, little girl, what have I done,
That makes you treat me so?
You caused me to weep, you caused me to mourn,
You caused me to leave my home.

Chords and Music Theory

Each of the basic chords you're learning (A, B C, D, etc.) are made up of the first, third, and fifth notes of the corresponding major scale. The C chord is made up of the first, third, and fifth notes of the C major scale and those notes are C, E, and G. The G chord is made up of the first, third, and fifth notes of the G major scale and those notes are G, B, and D. We can think of that (1, 3, 5) as the recipe for a major chord. Since it has three notes, it's called a "triad." All the chords you've learned so far, with the exception of the B7, are triads and more specifically "major triads." There are corresponding chords for every note on your fretboard or on the piano keyboard. Eventually we'll learn some sharp and flat chords.

On the mandolin, we often play four note chords where one of the three scale notes (1, 3, 5) may be repeated. Sometimes we'll play three string chords and we may not even play all three of the chord tones! Realistically speaking, we're limited to a maximum of four chord tones on the mandolin since the mandolin only has four strings. (Remember: we refer to each pair tuned in unison as one string.) I say "realistically" because it is possible to "split strings" and play two different notes by fretting at two different places on one string pair. Try it. It's possible but difficult.

So, what are all these other chord symbols we see all the time? C7, Gm, B♭6, Fm7, Dm9, etc.? Just like the basic three note chord or triad (G, C, D, etc.) had the recipe of 1, 3, 5 of the corresponding major scale, each of these, C7, Gm, B♭6, Fm7, Dm9, has it's own unique recipe.

When we see the numeral "7" after a letter like this: B7, G7, B♭7 E♭7, that chord has the recipe 1, 3, 5, ♭7 ("flat 7") of the corresponding major scale. In the C7 chord, which is also called a "C dominant 7," we use the basic C triad and add the flatted 7th note of the C scale. When we flat a note, we lower it by one half step or, on the mandolin, one fret. Thus C7 is made up of the notes C, E, G,

Bb; 1, 3, 5, b7 of the C major scale. Dominant seventh chords are four note chords. The B7 from "In the Pines" has the 1, 3, and 5 notes of the B major scale plus the flatted 7th note. B7 is a four note chord (1, 3, 5, b7 of the B major scale) with the notes B, D#, F#, A.

You don't have to be too concerned about all this music theory. At this point it's more important for you to memorize how to make all these chords on the mandolin and to recognize the shapes. Eventually you'll compare the shapes of similarly named chords (G, G7, Gm, Gm7) and realize that by modifying the shape you are bringing another chord recipe into play. Keep in mind that chord recipes and shapes are related as are similarly named chords.

Next we'll learn some minor chords. Let's look at the Gm or "G minor" chord below. To make a minor chord we take the basic major triad and change it as follows. Instead of 1, 3, 5, the minor chord, called a "minor triad," has 1, b3 ("flat 3"), 5 of the corresponding major scale. The chord diagrams will reflect that change. Compare them below.

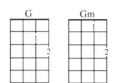

The names of the individual chords define the recipe of that chord and tell you what notes they contain. You already know that "C" means a basic triad with the 1, 3, 5 notes of the C major scale (C, E, G); "C7" means a dominant seventh chord with the 1, 3, 5, b7 notes of the C major scale (C, E, G, Bb); "Cm" means a minor triad with the 1, b3, 5 notes of the C major scale (C, Eb, G). Along those same lines, an E6 will be made up of the 1, 3, 5 and 6th notes of the E major scale. We can also mix majors, minors, and suffix numbers. For example, Am7 will include the 1, b3, 5, b7 of the A major scale.

In addition to the Gm, "St. James Infirmary" also has a Cm and a D7.

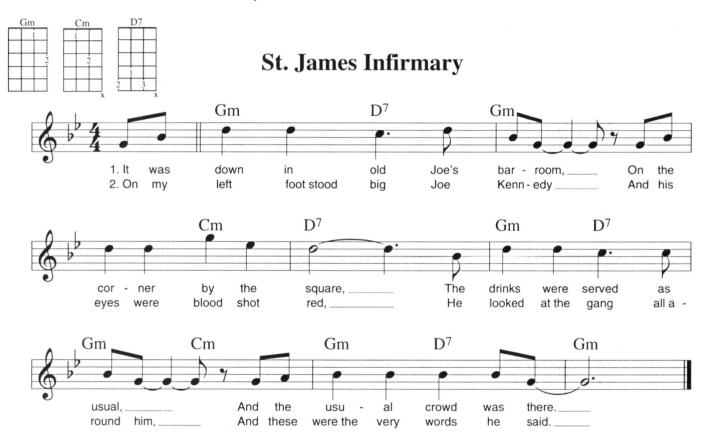

St. James Infirmary

1. It was down in old Joe's bar-room, _____ On the
2. On my left foot stood big Joe Kenn-edy _____ And his

cor - ner by the square, _____ The drinks were served as
eyes were blood shot red, _____ He looked at the gang all a -

usual, _____ And the usu - al crowd was there. _____
round him, _____ And these were the very words he said. _____

     Gm   D7   Gm
3. I went down to the St. James Infirmary,
     Cm D7
I saw my baby there,
     Gm   D7   Gm Cm
She was stretched out on a long, white table,
     Gm   D7   Gm
So cold, so pale, so fair.

4. Let her go, let her go, God bless her,
Wherever she may be.
She can ramble this wide world over,
And never find another man like me.

5. Now when I die please bury me,
In my high top Stetson hat,
Just put a twenty dollar gold piece on my watch chain,
So the gang will know I'm standing pat.

6. I want six crap shooters for my pall bearers,
And a chorus girl to sing me a song,
Put a jazz band on my hearse wagon,
Just to raise hell as we roll along.

7. And now that you have heard my story,
I'll take another shot of booze,
If anyone should happen to ask you,
Well, I've got the gambler's blues.

"Poor Wayfaring Stranger" uses a new Em and Am. Add finger 2 on the Em, finger 3 on the Am if you have to.

Poor Wayfaring Stranger

"John Henry" uses the Bb and F7 chords. Neither have any open or unfretted strings. You've had a few like this before (E, A, D7, Am, B7, etc.) and the amazing thing about "closed position" chords is that they are moveable up and down the fretboard. At each new position, they become a different chord. For example, play the Bb one fret lower (move it toward the nut) and the chord will be the A chord you learned for "Billy Boy." Move the F7 one fret down and it becomes an E7. Move the F7 up one fret (toward the bridge) and it will become an F#7.

From this point on we'll also start writing our chord diagrams a bit differently. In the B♭ chord shown below, the first finger frets strings three and four at the third fret. In the F7, the first finger frets the third string in the seventh fret. Instead of the terms "3rd fret" or "7th fret," you'll usually see the fret identified by simply a small number to the right of the chord diagram. (See both examples below.)

John Henry

1. When John Hen - ry was a lit - tle ba - by, _____ Just a -
2. John ___ Hen - ry had a lit - tle wo - man, _____ And her

sitting on his pap - py's knee, _____ Well he
name ___ was Pol - ly Anne, _____ John ___

picked up a ham - mer and a lit - tle piece of steel, Said "That
Hen - ry took sick ___ and he had to go to bed, Pol - ly

ham - mer's gon - na be the death of me, Lord, Lord,
Anne ___ drove ___ steel ___ like a man, Lord, Lord, Polly

Ham - mer's gon - na be the death of me." _____
Anne ___ drove ___ steel ___ like a man. _____

B♭
3. Captain said to John Henry,
           F7
"Gonna bring me a steam drill 'round,
    B♭
Gonna take that steam drill out on the job,
Gonna whop that steel on down,
           F7   B♭
Lawd, Lawd, gonna whop that steel on down."

4. John Henry told his captain,
Said, "A man ain't nothin' but a man,
And before I'd let that steam drill beat me down,
I'll die with this hammer in my hand,
Lawd, Lawd, I'll die with the hammer in my hand."

5. Oh the captain told John Henry,
"I believe this mountain's caving in,"
John Henry said to his captain, "Oh my,
It's my hammer just a'sucking wind,
Lawd, Lawd, it's my hammer just a'sucking wind."

6. John Henry told his captain,
"Looky yonder what I see,
Your drill's done broke and your hole's done choke,
And you can't drive steel like me,
Lawd, Lawd, and you can't drive steel like me."

7. John Henry was hammerin' on the mountain,
And his hammer was striking fire,
He drove so hard till he broke his poor heart,
And he laid down his hammer and he died,
Lawd, Lawd, laid down his hammer and he died.

8. They took John Henry to the graveyard,
And they buried him in the sand,
An every locomotive come roaring by,
Says, "Yonder lies a steel driving man,"
Lawd, Lawd, says, "Yonder lies a steel driving man."

15

To illustrate the moveable nature of these chords, let's move the B♭ and the F7 up one fret to make B and F#7 chords and learn a new song.

My Home's Across the Blue Ridge Mountains

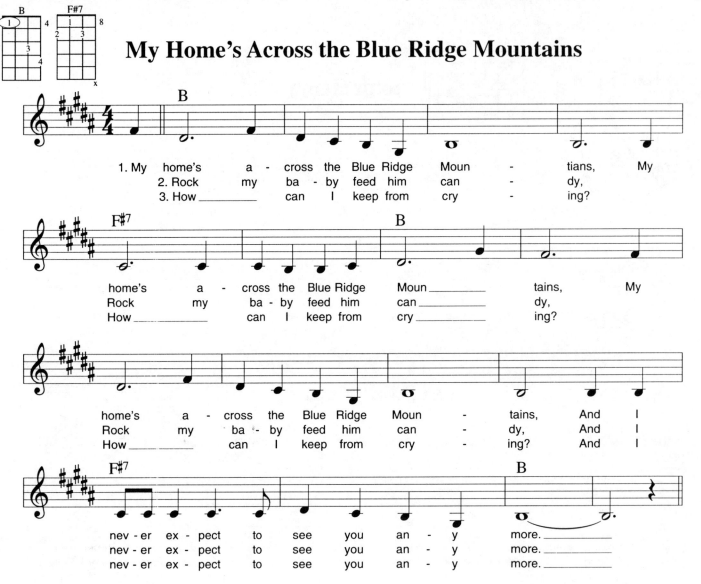

1. My home's a - cross the Blue Ridge Moun - tians, My
2. Rock my ba - by feed him can - dy,
3. How _____ can I keep from cry - ing?

home's a - cross the Blue Ridge Moun _____ tains, My
Rock my ba - by feed him can _____ dy,
How _____ can I keep from cry _____ ing?

home's a - cross the Blue Ridge Moun - tains, And I
Rock my ba - by feed him can - dy, And I
How _____ can I keep from cry - ing? And I

nev - er ex - pect to see you an - y more. _____
nev - er ex - pect to see you an - y more. _____
nev - er ex - pect to see you an - y more. _____

To exercise our fingers and ears with dominant seventh chords, we'll learn "Seventh Blues" with the A7, D7, and E7 chords.

Seventh Blues

by Dix Bruce

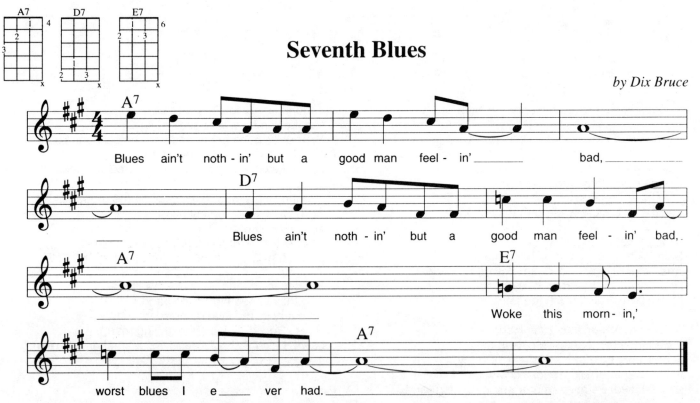

Blues ain't noth - in' but a good man feel - in' _____ bad, _____

_____ Blues ain't noth - in' but a good man feel - in' bad,

_____ Woke this morn - in,'

worst blues I e _____ ver had. _____

16

"Go Down Moses" uses new Dm and A7 chords along with the Gm you already know. This A7 is different from the one you just learned. It's the same chord, it's just played in a different position on the fingerboard. Why learn more than one chord form? Each form has its own distinctive sound and one may also be easier to reach than another. Our goal is to move our fretting hand as little as possible.

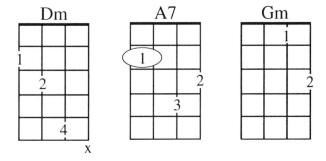

Go Down Moses

1. When Is-real was in Egy-pt's land, Let my peo-ple go, O -
2. "Thus saith the Lord," bold Mos-es said, Let my peo-ple go, "If

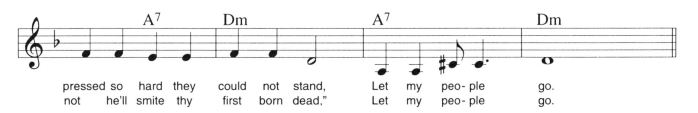

pressed so hard they could not stand, Let my peo-ple go.
not he'll smite thy first born dead," Let my peo-ple go.

Go down, Mos - es way down in Egy-pt land,_____

Tell__ old_____ phar__ oah,_____ "Let my peo-ple go!"

| Dm   A7   Dm
3. No more shall they in bondage toil,
A7   Dm
Let my people go,
      Dm   A7   Dm
Let them come out with Egypt's spoil,
A7   Dm
Let my people go.

4. The Lord told Moses what to do,
To lead the Hebrew children through.

5. As Israel stood by the waterside,
At God's command it did divide.

6. When they reached the other shore,
They sang a song of triumph o'er.

7. Pharaoh said he'd go across
But Pharaoh and his host were lost.

"Sometimes I Feel Like a Motherless Child" uses new Bm and Em chord along with the F#7 you learned on "My Home's Across the Blue Ridge Mountains."

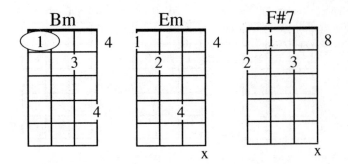

Sometimes I Feel Like a Motherless Child

     Bm
3. Sometimes I feel like a feather in the air,
     Em
Sometimes I feel like a feather in the air,
     Bm
Sometimes I feel like a feather in the air,
F#7   Bm   F#7   Bm
A long ways from home, a long ways from home,

Moving Closed Position Chords

At this point in the book you have learned to play almost all of the most important common forms of the major, minor, and dominant seventh chords. All are listed alphabetically in the chord dictionary in the back of this book. Remember that all the "closed position" chords, that is, chords which have no "open" or unfretted notes, are moveable up and down the fingerboard. To understand how that works, you have to understand a little bit about the "chromatic scale." The chromatic scale encompasses every consecutive note on your fretboard or on the piano keyboard. The notes of the ascending chromatic scale are:

A, A♯/B♭, B, C, C♯/D♭, D, D♯/E♭, E, F, F♯/G♭, G, G♯/A♭.

Notes listed with slashes in between ("C♯/D♭") are the same note with two different "enharmonic" names. There are no extra sharps or flats between E and F or B and C. Here's how we can use this information to move chords up and down the fingerboard.

Play the Bm chord from "Sometimes I Feel Like a Motherless Child" at its usual place. Now move the chord form up ("up" in pitch and toward the bridge of the mandolin) one fret. What is the name of this new chord? Look at the listing of the chromatic scale above. The next letter to the right (ascending) of the B is a C, so the new chord is a Cm.

Make the Bm again at its usual place and this time move the chord form down ("down" in pitch and toward the tuning pegs of the mandolin) one fret. Again, look at the chromatic scale above. The next letter to the left (descending) of the B is a B♭/A♯ ("B flat/A sharp"), so the new chord is called B♭m or A♯m.

Let's try the same exercise with the F♯7 chord. (Remember, you can also refer to this chord by its enharmonic name: G♭7.) Make it in its usual place and then move it up one fret. What's the new chord? If you said G7, you are correct. Once again, make the F♯7 and this time move it down one fret. What's the new chord? Right, it's F7.

I can't stress enough how important and valuable this is. If you understand these concepts and know just a few chord forms, you can move them all over the fingerboard and find virtually any chord. What a great little instrument! Reason #2!

Playing Melodies

Now that you have a solid background in chords, it's time to learn to play some simple melodies on the mandolin. We'll use tablature, which we'll explore shortly. But before we do that, let's make ourselves familiar with the rudiments of written music.

Written music communicates two things to the reader/player through notes: *pitch* and *rhythm*. Pitch tells us which sound or note to play, high or low. Rhythm tells us how long to hold that sound. Notes for the mandolin are written on a *staff* called the *treble clef,* which is identified by the *treble clef sign.*

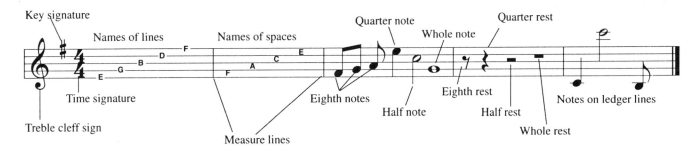

The staff has five lines and four spaces and each represents a different note. The notes on the lines, bottom to top are E, G, B, D, and F and can be remembered with the phrase "Every Good Boy Does Fine." The notes on the spaces, bottom to top are F, A, C, and E and spell out the word "**FACE.**"

The key signature, sharp (♯) or flat (♭) signs on a line or space change every occurrence of a note on that line or space by one half step. A sharp (♯) will raise a note one half step or one fret, a flat (♭) will lower a note by one half step or one fret. The time signature tells us how many beats there will be in each measure, which is the space enclosed by two vertical or measure lines. Common time signatures include 4/4 ("four four") and 3/4 ("three four").

The musical alphabet goes from A to G and notes on the staff, (line, space, line, space, etc.), ascend alphabetically A to G. They descend in reverse alphabetical order. If you know any note on a line or space, you can name any other by simply following up or down in alphabetical order.

Notes higher or lower than those on the staff are placed on extensions called *ledger lines.* Notes on ledger lines continue the alphabetical pattern above and below the staff. (See notes G, A, B, C, far left above; notes A, B, C far right above.)

As I mentioned before, the placement of notes on the staff, line or space, tells us the *pitch*, or how high or low, the note is. The different kinds of notes, eighth, quarter, half, whole, tell us how long to sound the pitch. Rests tell us when not to play and each note value has a corresponding rest, e.g. quarter, whole, half, eighth, rest.

Open or unfretted strings on the mandolin are tuned to the notes E (string 1-highest pitched), A (string 2), D (string 3) and G (string 4-lowest pitched). The diagram below shows where these notes are placed on the staff.

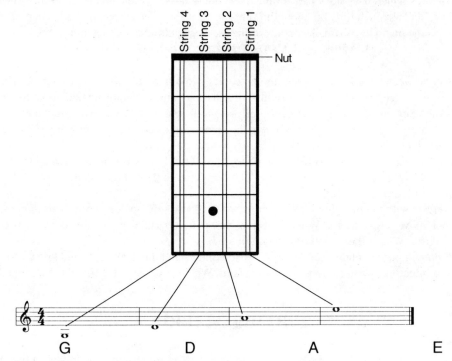

Other notes are made by fingering the strings at the different frets. The range of the mandolin is about three and one half octaves from the open fourth string G to the twentieth fret first string C. An octave is the interval from one note to the next occurrence of the same note above or below, for example from the mandolin's open fourth string G to the next G at the third string fifth fret. Your mandolin may have a few notes more or less depending upon the length of your fingerboard and the number of reachable frets. The staff and fret chart below shows where every note on the four strings from open strings to the twelfth fret octaves is located. Study a section of four or five frets at a time and familiarize yourself with the notes on every string. Try to relate each fret/string combination both with a line or space and a letter name. Play the note, repeat its position, (e.g. "first string, second fret"), then name it ("F-sharp"). Tablature locations are also shown. We'll explore tablature next.

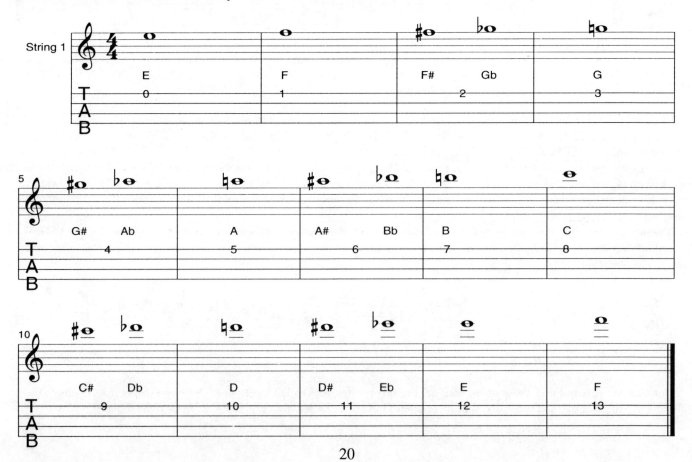

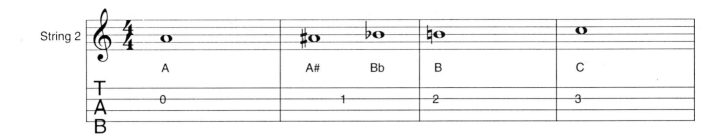

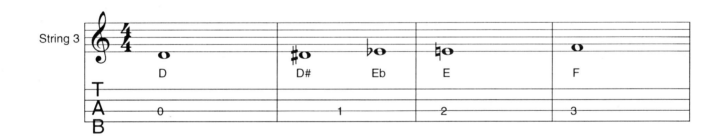

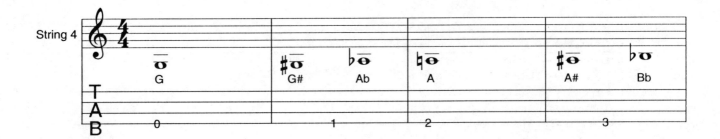

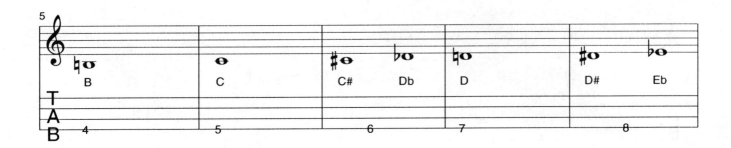

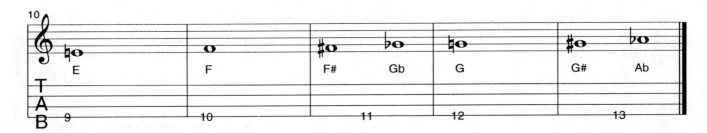

As I mentioned earlier, we'll use tablature to help you learn to play melodies quickly. The idea is to read the tablature, listen to the CD, and play along. The music will look similar to what you've seen so far except that we'll add a tablature line below the standard music and lyrics. Tablature is an alternative to music reading that shows the position of a note on the fingerboard. Numbers, which correspond to the fret where the note is played, are arranged on a four line staff, each line representing one of the strings on the mandolin. Rather than reading notes, the player reads positions. The top line of the tablature staff represents the first or highest pitched string (E) of the mandolin, second from the top is the second string (A), third from the top is the third string (D), and the bottom line is the fourth string (G).

A zero on any of the lines means to play that string unfretted or open. If you see a numeral "1" put your fretting finger on that fret and pick the note, and so on. The italic numbers directly above or below the tablature line tell you which fretting hand finger to use to fret a note. You'll see quite a few of these finger notations in the first few songs. After that, if a melody note repeats, we'll leave out the fretting finger designation for the sake of clarity in the music. Eventually we'll leave them out altogether, unless there's an unusual fingering I want to point out, and you'll be able to figure them out for yourself.

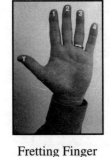

Fretting Finger Numbers

In the example below we see the melody and chords to "Camptown Races" shown in standard notation. Below the music staff you'll find the corresponding tablature staff. The first two G notes are played at the fifth fret of the third string. The next note, an E, is played at the second fret of the third string. This is followed by another G. In the next measure, the first note is an A, played on the open second string. Fretting finger numbers are shown in italics below the lyrics and above the tablature staff. We're suddenly swimming in numbers here so don't get confused. Remember that the tablature numbers are on the horizontal lines. Fretting finger numbers are above the lines and shown in italics. Try playing along with the recorded version.

Tablature is a great tool for learning melodies quickly, especially if you don't know how to read music or don't know how to read music on the mandolin. These days tablature is widely available in music of many styles. Eventually you'll want to learn to read notes to enable you to read any kind of music on the mandolin, not just music with mandolin tablature. Again, I suggest my "You Can Teach Yourself Mandolin" as a good place to start with basic music reading.

Since you already know the first four measures of "Camptown Races," let's make it our first song! Pick the individual notes with a single downward stroke. It may help your accuracy to brush the pickguard or top of the mandolin with the fourth finger of your picking hand. A controversy rages as to whether to do it or not. Proponents say that it increases accuracy; opponents say the may ultimately slow a player down, especially if the pinkie gets planted on the top of the mandolin. See the photos. Go for smooth transitions between notes. It'll take a lot of practice, but the results will make it well worth the time. Listen to the "First Melody" track on the CD.

Picking–No pinkie

Picking–Pinkie Brush

Camptown Races

Key of C

Stephen Foster

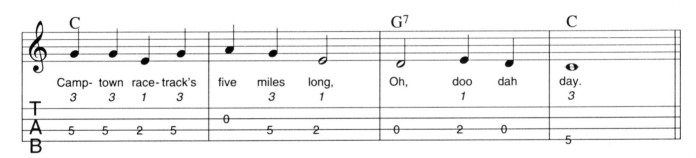

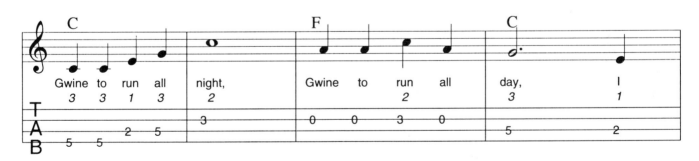

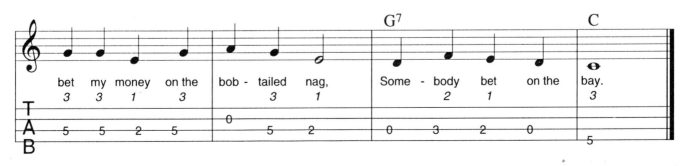

The songs you are learning are in a variety of different keys. "Camptown Races" is in the key of C; "Just a Closer Walk With Thee" is in the key of G; "The Great Speckled Bird" is in the key of A; "Lonesome Valley" is in the key of F. (Keys are noted in the upper left hand corner of the music.) Keys are defined by their corresponding major scale, the familiar "do-re-me-fa-sol-la-ti-do." So, the C major scale defines the key of C; the G major scale defines the key of G, etc. The different keys and scales use different notes and chords, as you'll see as you progress through these songs. The same song can be played in a variety of keys to accommodate different instruments or vocal ranges. For example, I have a pretty typical male voice and if I sing something in the key of C, a typical female voice might need to sing it in the key of F or G. For more info on scales and keys, check out my book "Guide to Capo, Transposing, & the Nashville Numbering System." (MB98413)

Just a Closer Walk With Thee

Key of G

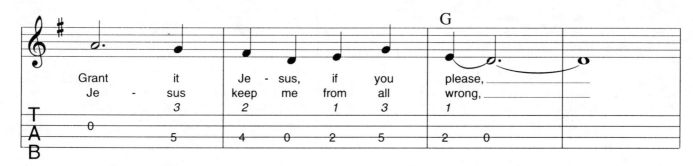

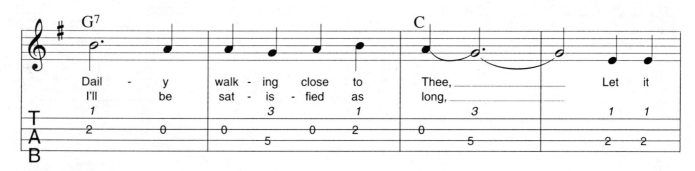

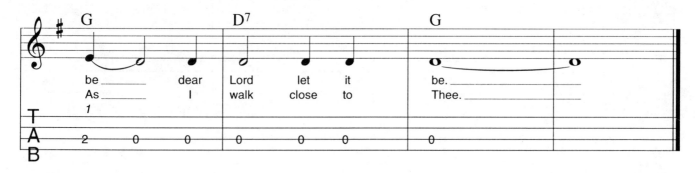

24

My Walking Cane

Key of D

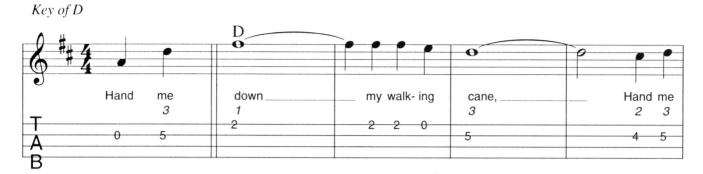

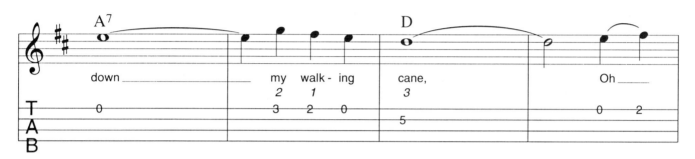

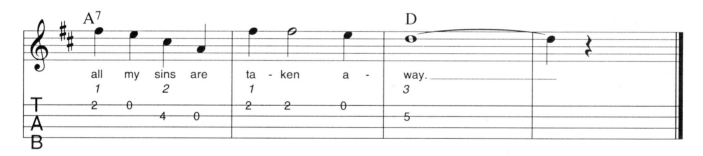

          D
2. Oh, hand me down my bottle of corn,
         A7   D
Oh, hand me down my bottle of corn,
             G
Oh, hand me down my bottle of corn,
         D
I'll get drunk as sure's you're born,
   A7   D
For all my sins are taken away.

3. Oh, I got drunk and I landed in jail,
And there wasn't no one to go my bail.

4. The meat is tough, and the beans are bad,
Oh, my God, I can't eat that.

5. The devil chased me 'round a stump,
I thought he'd catch me at every jump.

The Great Speckled Bird

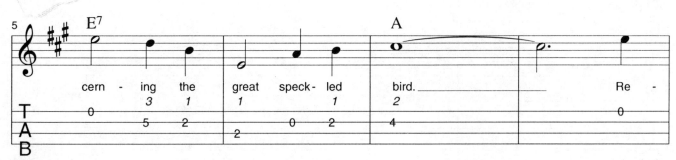

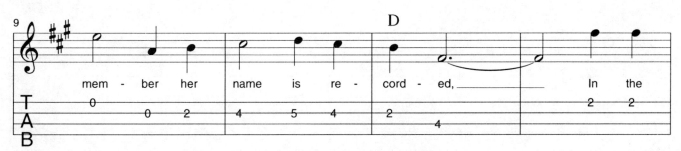

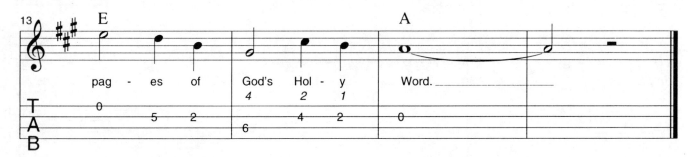

2. Desiring to lower her standard,
    A   D
    E7   A
They watch every move that she makes.
                         D
They try to find fault with her teachings.
    E7   A
But really they find no mistake.

3. She is spreading her wings for a journey,
She's going to leave by and by.
When the trumpet shall sound in the morning
She'll rise and go up in the sky.

4. In the presence of all her despisers,
With a song never uttered before,
She will rise and be gone in a moment,
'Till the great tribulation is o'er.

5. I am glad I have learned of her meekness.
I am glad that my name's in her book,
And I want to be one never fearing
On the face of my Saviour to look.

Lonesome Valley

Key of F

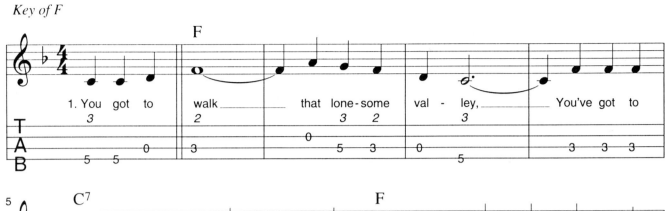

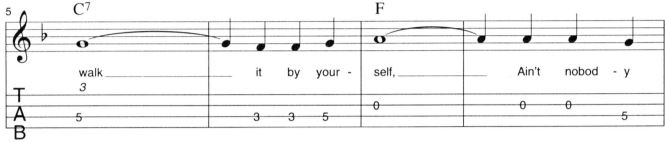

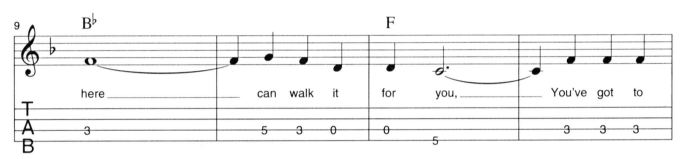

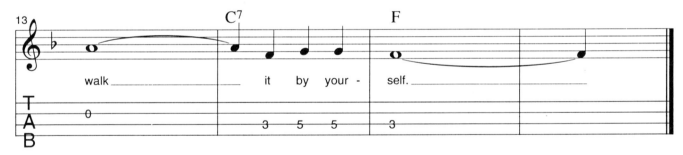

F

2. Mother's got to walk that lonesome valley, etc.

      C7   F

She's got to walk it by herself,

       B♭   F

Ain't nobody here can walk it for her,

        C7   F

She's got to walk it by herself.

Sister's got to walk, etc., Brother, Father.

Up to now, all the songs we've worked with have used quarter, half, and whole notes, which we've played with a single down stroke of the pick. The next song, "Buffalo Gals" introduces eighth notes. Two eighth notes fit in the time of one quarter note and we play two consecutive eighth notes with a down and an up stroke of the pick. We'll note these in the music with arrows: ↓ = down stroke; ↑ = up stroke. Again, you'll find a lot of arrows in these first songs, then less as you get more experience playing with up and down strokes. Because of the arrows, some of the fretting hand finger numbers have been moved below the tablature staff. Listen to the "Eighth Notes" track on the CD.

Buffalo Gals

Key of C

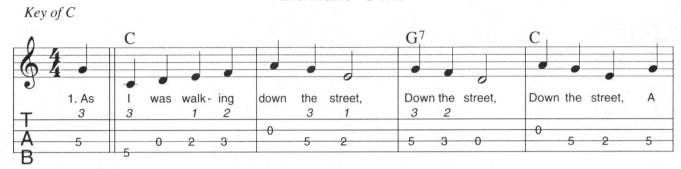

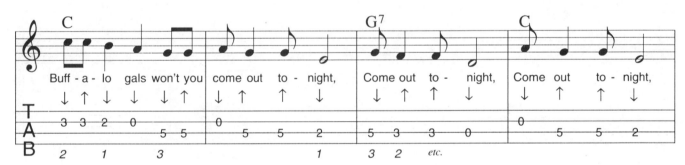

Fretting finger numbers:

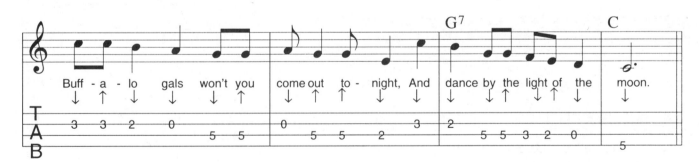

Bluegrass

Since most mandolinists in the world today probably play in bluegrass bands, we'll spend the next few pages exploring bluegrass music.

"Oh, Them Golden Slippers" is a tune played in bluegrass and old time bands. I've written it with just a few of the pick direction/arrow notations shown. As the rhythms of the melody repeat, so do the patterns of pick direction. In an effort to simplify the music, I've only shown the patterns the first time they occur. If you get stuck, refer to the previous passage.

The first part of this song repeats, as shown by the double bar & dots in measures 1 and 8. Play this part twice and then go on to part two, which does not repeat. (See next page.)

28

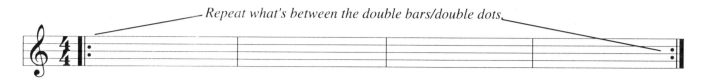

Oh, Them Golden Slippers

Mandolinists in bluegrass bands play lots of fiddle tunes. Here's one of the most popular, "Soldier's Joy." Watch your pick direction on the eighth notes. Each part of "Soldier's Joy" repeats and has first and second endings. The first time through part one, play the first ending, repeat part one, skip the first ending, play the second ending, then go on to part two. For more practice with fiddle tunes, I suggest my **BackUP TRAX: Old Time & Fiddle Tunes** (MB94339BCD). It's a book/CD set where you play along, at slow and regular speeds, with a recorded band. You can practice rhythm, lead, and improvisation. You play all the solos and the band backs you up! Check it out on my website: musicnow.com.

Soldier's Joy

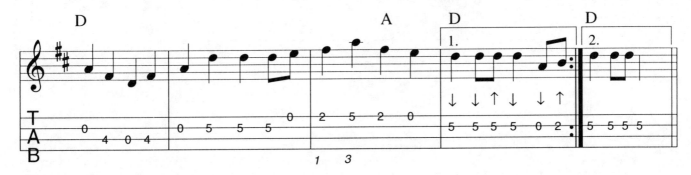

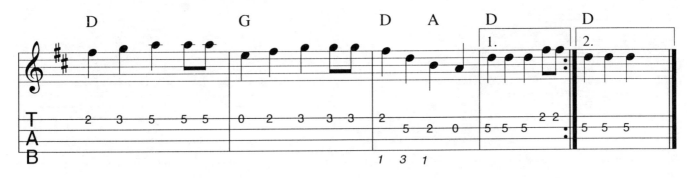

"East Virginia Blues" is another bluegrass classic. We'll use it to demonstrate a technique virtually all bluegrass mandolinists use in the style. If you look at the first version of the song below, you'll notice that it has lots of notes that are held for a long time. For example, the note over the word "born" in measure one is held for five beats. Up until now you've played a note like this with one pick stroke. In a bluegrass band situation, the sound of the note will probably die out long before five beats. So, mandolinists add extras notes to fill in. See the example below and listen to it and the two versions of "East Virginia Blues" on the CD.

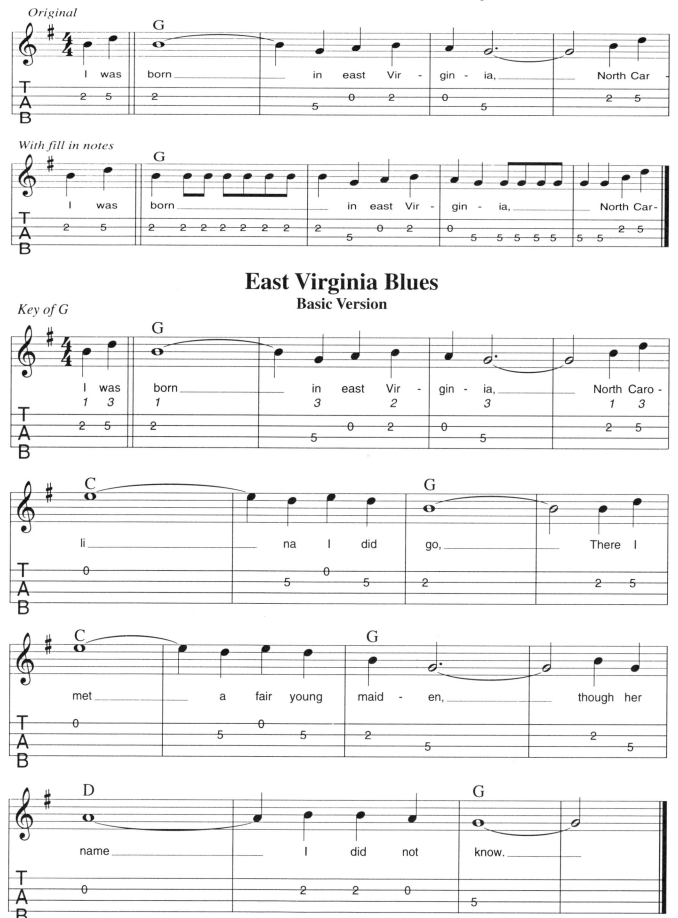

East Virginia Blues
Basic Version

31

<pre>
                    G
2. Oh, her hair was dark and curly,
          C   G
And her cheeks were rosy red,
          C   G
On her breast she wore white linen,
          D   G
Where I longed to lay my head.
</pre>

<pre>
3. Molly dear, go ask your mother,
If my bride you'll ever be,
If she says no, come back and tell me,
And I'll run away with thee.

4. No I'll not go ask my mother,
Where she lies on her bed of rest,
For in her hand she holds a dagger,
To kill the man that I love best.
</pre>

East Virginia Blues

Key of G

(Note fill in version)

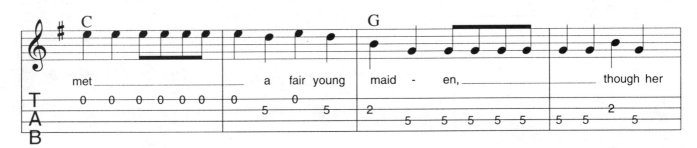

<pre>
5. I don't want your green back dollar,
I don't want your watch and chain,
All I want is you my darling,
Say you'll take me back again,

6. The ocean's deep and I can't wade it,
And I have no wings to fly,
I'll just get some blue-eyed boatman,
For to row me o'er the tide.
</pre>

<pre>
7. I'll go back to East Virginia,
North Carolina ain't my home,
I'll go back to East Virginia,
Leave old North Carolina alone.

8. Oh you know I'd like to see you,
At my door you're welcome in,
At my gate I'll always greet you,
For you're the girl I tried to win.
</pre>

"Roving Gambler" is another song that uses the note fill in technique. This one's in a new key: B♭.

Roving Gambler

Key of B♭

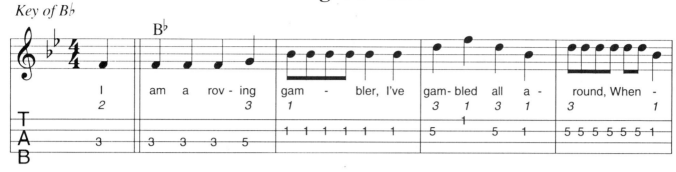

I am a rov-ing gam - bler, I've gam-bled all a - round, When-

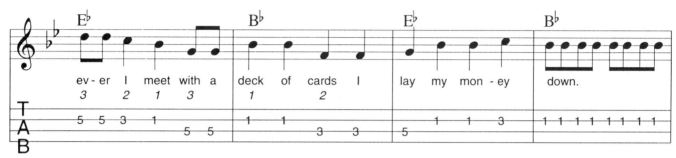

ev-er I meet with a deck of cards I lay my mon-ey down.

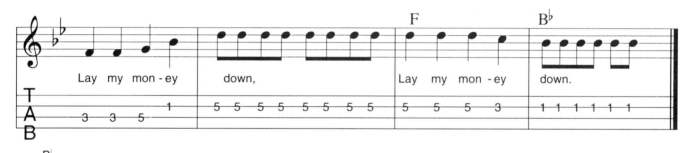

Lay my mon-ey down, Lay my mon-ey down.

B♭
2. I've gambled down in Washington, I've gambled over in Spain,
E♭   B♭   F   B♭
I'm on my way to Georgia to gamble my last game.
                              F   B♭
Gamble my last game, gamble my last game.

3. I had not been in Frisco many more weeks than three,
I met up with a pretty little girl, she fell in love with me.
Fell in love with me, fell in love with me.

4. She took me in her parlor, she cooled me with her fan,
She whispered low in her mother's ear, "I love this gambling man.
Love this gambling man, love this gambling man."

5. "Oh, daughter, oh, dear daughter, how can you treat me so,
To leave your dear old mother and with the gambler go?
With the gambler go, with the gambler go?"

6. "Oh, mother, oh, dear mother, you know I love you well,
But the love I feel for the gambling man, no human tongue can tell.
No human tongue can tell, human tongue can tell."

7. "Oh, mother, oh, dear mother, I'll tell you if I can,
If you ever see me coming back again, I'll be with the gambling man.
With the gambling man, with the gambling man."

Great Big Bad Bluegrass Chop Chords

Bluegrass mandolinists use different types of chords than you've learned thus far. In a bluegrass band, the mandolinist plays several roles: 1) lead soloist playing melodies; 2) accompanist playing chords; 3) "drummer" playing solid rhythmic backbeats. We've already addressed roles 1) and 2), now here's 3). Listen to a demonstration of the chop chord on the "Bluegrass Chop" track on the CD.

The chords you know often include open string (unfretted) notes. When we strum chords like this, they ring for a long time. In order to play a backbeat, like a snare drum, we need to be able to choke off that sound and emphasize it's rhythmic rather than harmonic content. So, we use chords where all the notes are fretted. The technique involves a kind of pulse with our fretting hand. We press down as usual to sound the chord, then relax that grip just enough to mute the strings and stop the sound. Don't lift your fingers off the strings altogether but rather pulse your fretting hand. Listen to the examples on the CD.

At first glance, whether you're looking at a chord grid or a photo of a fretting hand, these chords look impossibly difficult. No doubt about it, they are tough. It just takes time and practice. The good news is that since these chord forms are in closed (all strings fretted) positions, they are moveable all over the fingerboard. Learn one form and you can move it to at least ten other positions to play ten other chords!

Here are the A, D, and E7 bluegrass chop chords. Try them out on "Roll in My Sweet Baby's Arms." The small "x" under string 1 on the D and E7 means to not play it. Damp it with the inside of your fretting hand fingers. (See next page.)

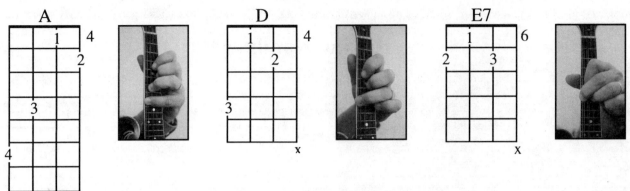

Roll in My Sweet Baby's Arms

A
3. Sometimes there's a change in the weather,
                              E7
Sometimes there's a change in the sea,
      A   D
Sometimes there's a change in my own true love,
      E7   A
But there's never no change in me.

4. Mama's a ginger-cake baker,
Sister can weave and can spin,
Dad's got an interest in that old cotton mill,
Just watch that old money roll in.

5. They tell me that your parents don't like me,
They drove me away from your door,
If I had all my life to live over,
I would never go there anymore.

6. Now where were you last Friday night,
While I was lying down in jail?
Walking the streets with another man,
Wouldn't even go my bail.

Now let's put the great advantage of closed position chords to work. We'll move all the chords in "Roll in My Sweet Baby's Arms" up (toward the bridge) one fret or 1/2 step to the key of B♭. The A chord becomes B♭; The D becomes E♭, the E7 becomes F7. (Remember that we can refer to these chords by their enharmonic names also: B♭ = A♯; E♭ = D♯; F♯7 = G♭7; A♭ = G♯; D♭ = C♯; E♭7 = D♯7.)

Once you feel comfortable doing that, move the chords up one more fret to the key of B. The B♭ chords becomes B; the E♭ becomes E, the F7 becomes F♯7. Of course you can go in the opposite direction too. Go back to the original key of A. Move each chord down one fret to the key of A♭. The A chords becomes A♭; The D becomes D♭, the E7 becomes E♭7. Is this cool or what? Be sure to practice "Roll in My Sweet Baby's Arms" in all the new keys. Chord grids are shown below.

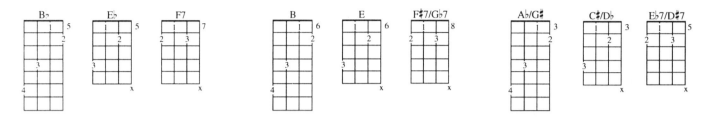

Before we move on and wrap things up, let's learn one more song with a slightly different arrangement of chop chords. Here's "This Train" in the key of D.

This Train

2. This train don't carry no gamblers, this train,
$\qquad\qquad\qquad$ A7
This train don't carry no gamblers, this train.
D
This train don't carry no gamblers,
G7
No hypocrites, no midnight ramblers,
D
This train is bound for glory, this train.

3. This train don't carry no liars, etc.
No hypocrites and no high flyers,
This train is bound for glory, this train.

4. This train don't carry no rustlers, etc.
No street walkers, no two-bit hustlers,
This train is bound for glory, this train.

Just as you did with "Roll in My Sweet Baby's Arms," move these chords around to different keys. First move all the chords up one fret, then down, and so on. When you feel really brave, move up and down by two, three, four, or more frets. Be sure to identify the new chord/key. Here are the chord sets with enharmonic names.

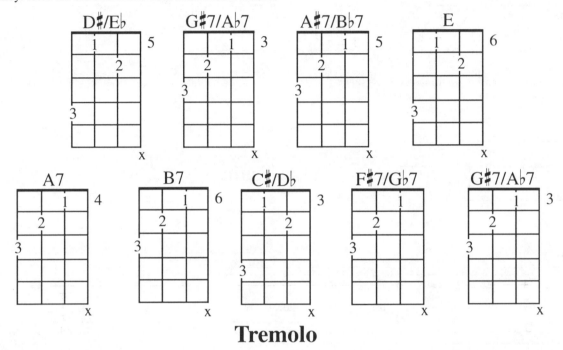

Tremolo

On "East Virginia Blues" and "Roving Gambler" we played a series of eighth notes to extend notes and keep the sound going. If we play even more notes to make a denser, more robust sound, it's called tremolo. Tremolo is a beautifully expressive technique and a must for the mandolinist to master. Listen to the examples on the CD and then try playing tremolo on "Greensleeves." We won't tremolo every note, only those longer than quarters. I've marked these notes on the first two staves with a slash. After that, you should be able to find your own way. Listen to the "Tremolo" example on the CD. In measure 29 you'll find a C chord in parenthesis. Some people play the C instead of the Em.

Greensleeves

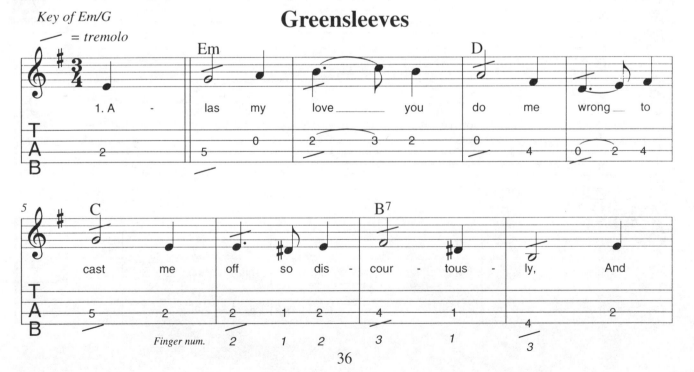

Chord Dictionary

Reminder: Closed position chords are moveable up and down the neck. The "r" under a chord grid shows where the chord's "root" is located. This root note names the chord and as you move a closed chord form, this note will identify and name the new chord.

Major Chords

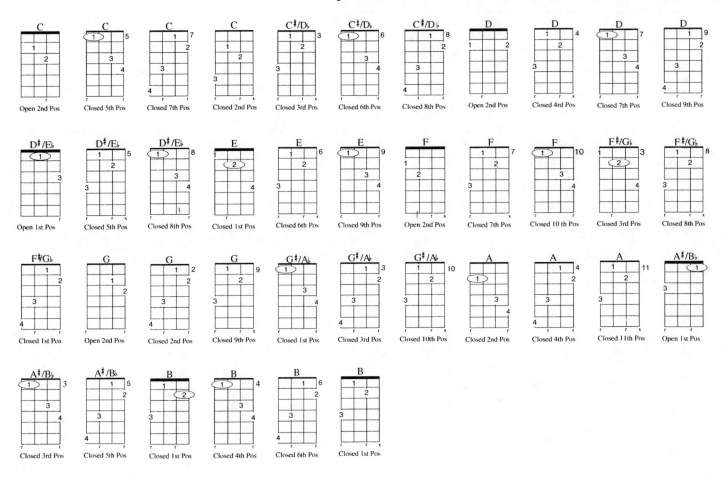

Minor Chords

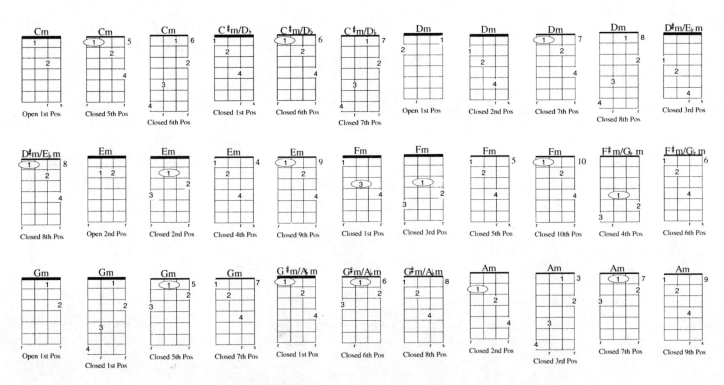

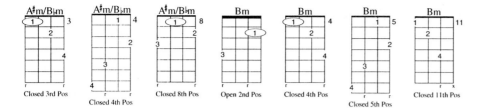

Dominant Seventh Chords

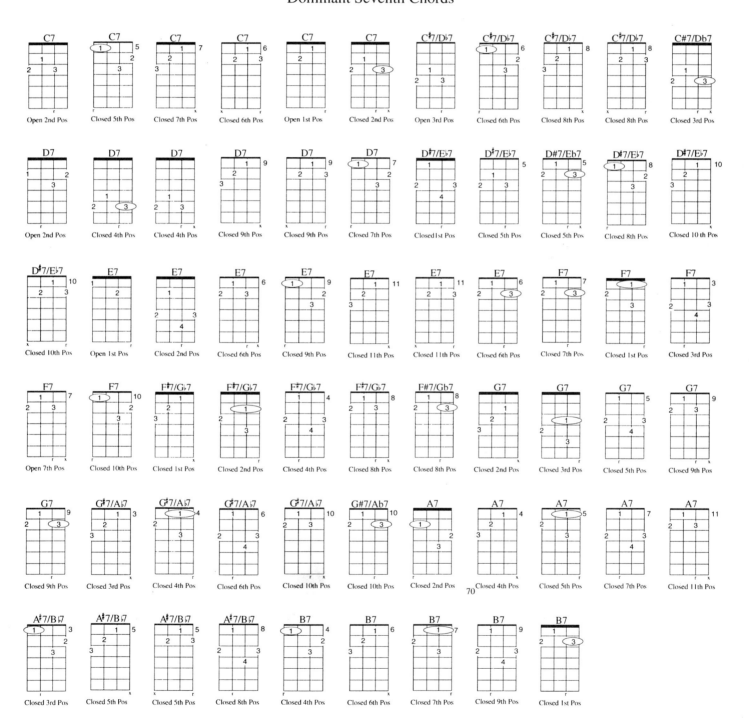

39

Wrapping Things Up

This brings us to the end of "First Lessons for Mandolin" and you've accomplished a great deal. You know a lot about the mandolin and its parts, you're mastering the art of tuning. You've learned all the important major, minor, and seventh chords and how to play them on twenty seven songs. (Don't forget the chord dictionary on the previous pages.) You've learned to play some basic melodies and to read tablature in the process. You've struggled with the seldom loved, always respected "Big Bad Bluegrass Chop Chord" and you understand how to move it and other closed position chords around to many different positions and chords up and down the neck. You can play in just about any key! Finally, you've begun to develop your tremolo on slow songs. Not bad, not bad at all! From here you can take your playing anywhere you want, to any style of music from bluegrass to classical, rock to jazz. You can read chords and learn songs and tunes from books, off the Internet, from recordings, live concerts, or friends around a campfire. The sky is truly the limit. Go back to the beginning of the book and try to play the melody to all the songs whose chords you already know. And, be sure to learn the chords to all the songs you learned leads for. Practice both chords and leads with the CD. Use the auto repeat function to work on something until you master it.

Check out my latest books, CDs, and videos at www.musixnow.com. Of course I wholeheartedly recommend the mandolin projects. No mando-home should be without them! Build your repertoire with my "Great Mandolin Pickin' Tunes" (MB98420BCD) book and CD set. Learn to play fiddle tunes with my "BackUP TRAX: Old Time & Fiddle Tunes." (MB94339BCD, CDB available January 2003) You'll jam along with a recorded band and you'll play all the leads. It's a great way to learn! If you're interested in swing music, you'll enjoy "BackUP TRAX: Swing & Jazz." (MB94344BCD) Don't forget my "You Can Teach Yourself Mandolin"! (MB94331) We also have back issues of "Mandolin World News."

I hope you'll stay in touch as you progress in your journey. I'll continue writing, recording, performing and learning right there with you. Here's wishing you all the best!

Dix Bruce
August 2002

Dix Bruce is a musician and writer from the San Francisco Bay Area. He has authored over thirty five books, recordings, and videos for Mel Bay Publications. He edited Mandolin World News, David Grisman's legendary mandolin magazine, from 1978 to 1984. Dix does studio work on guitar, mandolin, and banjo and has recorded two LPs with mandolin legend Frank Wakefield, eight big band CDs with the Royal Society Jazz Orchestra, his own collection of American folk songs entitled "My Folk Heart" on which he plays guitar, mandolin, autoharp and sings, and a CD of string swing & jazz entitled "Tuxedo Blues." He contributed two original compositions to the soundtrack of Harrod Blank's acclaimed documentary "Wild Wheels." He has released three CDs of traditional American songs and originals with guitarist Jim Nunally.

Dix Bruce arranged, composed, played mandolin, and recorded the music for the CD ROM computer game "The Streets of Sim City" for the Maxis Corporation. His mandolin music is featured on a virtual radio station within the game. You can also hear him on the soundtrack to "The Sims House Party."